JOURNEY
TO
THE BELOVED

Sufi Poems by
YUNUS EMRE

Translated by
Ersin Balcı

kopernik

JOURNEY
TO
THE BELOVED

Sufi Poems by

YUNUS EMRE

Kopernik

YUNUS EMRE, one of the pinnacles of Turkish sufi thought and Turkish poetry, lived in Anatolia in the last half of the 13th and in the first quarter of the 14th centuries. Despite his great reputation as a poet, very little is known about his life—almost nothing in fact. Where he was born, where and how he lived is mostly unknown.

Yunus Emre's works are collected into two books: *Divan and Risaletun Nushiyye (The Book of Admonitions)*. *Divan* of Yunus Emre compiles the poems he wrote throughout his sufi life. And *Risaletun Nushiyye* is a book of spiritual admonitions written in 1307 and is arranged in the *masnavi* poetry form. These didactic poems tell of a sufi's inner journey towards spiritual perfection.

ERSİN BALCI, the translator of *Journey to the Beloved*, was born in 1965 in Düzce, Turkey. He studied philosophy at the Middle East Technical University, Ankara. As to his professional career, he has been working as a consultant for the Turkish government for more than twenty years. He also served as a member of the Committee of Communication at the Turkish National Commission for UNESCO between 2014-2018.

He has translated the *Fusus al-Hikam* by Muhyiddin ibn Arabi and *The Way of Muhammad* by Abdalqadir as-Sufi into Turkish. He has also translated *The Architect of Love - Sufi Poems by Niyazi Mısri and Gather Sunlight for Me: A Selection of Modern Turkish Poetry* into English. He is the author of *Kendi Kitabını Oku (Read Your Own Book)*, a book on sufism, which he is now translating into English.

Published by Kopernik Inc.
®Ersin Balcı 2018

Editor-in-Chief: Abdülkadir Özkan
Advisor: Prof. Halil Berktay
Series Editor: Dr. Yaşar Çolak
Director: Cengiz Şişman
Copy Editing: Tim Thurston
Cover Design: Ali Kaya
Application:Sinopsis

Kopernik Publishing House
Kopernik Inc.
108 Olde Towne Avenue Unit: 308 Gaithersburg Maryland 20877 - USA
www.kopernikpublishing.com

Certification no: 35175
ISBN: 978-975-2439-98-6
First Edition: November 2018

Printed in ISTANBUL
Bilnet Matbaacılık ve Yayıncılık AŞ

ISTANBUL – LONDON – NEW YORK – WASHINGTON DC

JOURNEY
TO
THE BELOVED

Sufi Poems by
YUNUS EMRE

Translated by
Ersin Balcı

kopernik

JOURNEY
to
THE BELOVED

YUNUS EMRE

CONTENTS

PREFACE

"Know yourself." This has always been the call of wise men to all human beings for centuries. Although there is no distance, knowing ourselves is the longest and the hardest journey that we may ever experience. For we ourselves are the biggest puzzle to be solved.

Here in the world, we don't really know who we are, and what our relation is to the universe and to God. It's difficult for us to discern in which ways we are separate from and in which ways we are unified with the universe and with God.

In this search for the kernel of yourself, surprisingly, in the very depths of your existence there you find God. And in the course of this journey, Love emerges which takes you beyond even yourself. So your life becomes a journey to the Beloved—the very Beloved within yourself.

In this process, one has to "deconstruct" his own self, which is indeed but a fictional entity. And this very self is what hinders seeing Reality as it is. So, beyond our understanding of reality, we witness a totally different scene— where Man, the axis of the universe, is established at the very core of existence.

The Man, the perfected Man—the one who has realized himself—is where the puzzle is solved. He is the answer of all our questions. He is the only resting place on the troubled paths of the world. He is the final abode where one may arrive; the deep serenity we have been looking for.

Yunus Emre, the sufi poet, having accomplished his own journey, tells us about this in his poems.

In this book, we are presenting you 50 poems by Yunus Emre, rendered into English. We hope this selection of poems conveys the spirit of his poetry, his wisdom, and his love towards all humanity and all creation.

All his words shed a healing light onto our troubled and doubtful hearts. He says:

I have not come for selfish assertions,
My task is Love;
The heart is God's abode,
And I am here to build hearts.

Let's read. It is not just his story. He is indeed telling us about ourselves. This is our story.

ERSİN BALCI

INTRODUCTION

Yunus Emre is one of the pinnacles of Turkish sufi thought and Turkish poetry. He lived in Anatolia in the last half of the 13th and in the first quarter of the 14th centuries. Being a highly respected sufi poet throughout the centuries, today, his poems are still widely read and his deep love for God and humanity still resonates among people in Turkey. However, as the poems of Yunus Emre speak of perennial truths which shed light on all humanity, they are certainly beyond just being a part of Turkish culture: they are the inheritance of all humanity. And today, we see that his universal and humanitarian voice has reached beyond Turkish speaking communities, as has been witnessed when the year 1991 was announced by UNESCO as "International Yunus Emre Year" in commemoration of the 750th anniversary of his birth.

The Life of Yunus Emre

It is quite astonishing that, despite his great reputation as a poet, very little is known about his life—almost nothing in fact. So, we do not know where he was born, nor where and how he lived. Although there are various claims from dif-

ferent sources (which are but a handful of documents written about him) about such details, his life is still mostly unknown. However, the information, given in a manuscript at
the Beyazıt State Library in Istanbul, which states that he was
born in 1240 and died in 1320 at the age of 82 can be accepted
as true as it can be confirmed by the names and events mentioned by Yunus Emre in his poems. The well-known sufi
masters he mentions as his contemporaries (such as Mawlana Jalaluddin Rumi, Ahmed Fakih, Seydi Balim, and Geyikli
Baba) also lived in the same period.

This was a time when the Anatolian Seljuk State was dis-
solving into Turkish principalities, from which the Ottoman
Empire would grow. This period witnessed great turmoils:
Mongol raids and ransacks; rivalries and wars among principalities as well as widespread famine. In such a time of dis-
tress, sufi masters like Yunus Emre and Mawlana Jalaluddin
Rumi brought the Anatolian people who underwent great
miseries and bitter torment the hope for the future; healing
their wounded hearts.

There is also a discussion among scholars about wheth-
er Yunus Emre had a formal education or not. While some
scholars say that he was an uneducated man, others claim
that he did indeed have a formal *madrasa* education. Those
who want to picture him as a man of folk —which is indeed
true—tend to see him as an uneducated man. However, the
rich vocabulary and stylistic skills in his poems indicate that
he was, in fact, a learned man. So, he might have had a formal *madrasa* education. But, he might also had his education
in the sufi lodge where he spent several decades, bearing in
mind that sufi lodges have always been centers of education,
although not in a formal manner.

The Epic Life of Yunus Emre

While we know almost nothing about the historical Yunus Emre, there is an abundance of information about him in the epic stories of the sufis.

His story is told extensively in the *Vilayatnama of Hadji Bektash Veli* (*The Saintly Exploits of Hadji Bektash Veli*), a book which recounts the spiritual life of Hadji Bektash Veli, another Anatolian sufi of great renown. In this book, it is related that Yunus Emre met Hadji Bektash Veli and he sent him to Tapduk Emre for his spiritual training. As the legend goes, Yunus Emre served at the sufi lodge of Tapduk Emre for thirty years, everyday bringing wood on his back to the lodge from a nearby mountain. It's related that he never cut any twisted wood, saying, "That which is not straight does not suit a Friend of God."

Another source of information about Yunus Emre is *Vakiat-i Uftade.* In this book, Aziz Mahmud Hudayi, a disciple of Mehmed Uftade, a 16th century Anatolian sufi, relates stories he heard from his spiritual master. According to a story told in *Vakiat-i Uftade*, Yunus Emre, after serving thirty years, surmises he has failed in completing his spiritual inner journey and decides—in great desolation—to give up his spiritual training. So, he leaves the lodge in secrecy. However, upon experiencing some extraordinary spiritual events on the road, he understands that he miscomprehended his spiritual state and it was nothing but a mistake to leave the lodge:

> "Yunus Emre served Tapduk Emre for thirty years, yet nothing had been revealed to him from the unseen world. So he fled the lodge and ran away to desolate fields. One day he encountered seven dervishes and became friends with them. Every evening, one of them was praying, and with the power of his prayer, a divine table descended from heaven. The turn came to Yunus.

He, too, prayed: "O, God, do not let me be ashamed. For the sake of whom they are praying, for his mercy, please do not let me be ashamed." That evening two tables descended. The dervishes asked: "For whose mercy's sake did you pray?" Yunus said: "You first tell me yours." They said: "We pray for the mercy's sake of Yunus Emre who served Tapduk Emre for thirty years." Hearing this, he returned immediately to the lodge and and took sanctuary with Ana Baci, the wife of Tapduk Emre, imploring her: "O please, have him forgive me!" Ana Baci said: Tapduk goes out to take ablution for the morning prayer. Lay on the threshold of the door. When he steps on you, he will ask who it is in his way." I will answer, "It's Yunus". "If he asks: "Which Yunus?" know that you no longer have a place in his heart. But if he asks, "Is it our Yunus?" then, ask him to forgive you. Yunus did as Ana Baci instructed. As an old man, Tapduk Emre could not see well so Ana Baci was holding his arm, bringing him for his ablution. That morning on the threshold his foot touched Yunus. He asked who he was. Baci said that it was Yunus. Tapduk Emre asked "Is it our Yunus?"—upon which Yunus Emre pleaded to be forgiven."

The Works of Yunus Emre

Yunus Emre's works are collected into two books: *The Risaletun Nushiyye* and the *Divan*. *Risaletun Nushiyye (The Book of Admonitions)* is a book of spiritual admonitions written in 1307 and is arranged in the *masnavi* poetry form. These didactic poems tell of a sufi's inner journey towards spiritual perfection.

Divan of Yunus Emre compiles the poems he wrote throughout his sufi life. Although there isn't any single manuscript of his *Divan* that survives from his time, there are some reliable extant manuscript copies at hand which were copied in the 15th or 16th centuries.

In this present book, the 50 Yunus Emre poems rendered into English are selected from the critical edition of the *Divan* of Yunus Emre, prepared by Prof. Dr. Mustafa Tatcı, a scholar who has worked extensively on Yunus Emre and his poems. This *Divan* prepared by Tatçı includes 417 poems.

The Other Yunus Emre

There is also another poet whose name is also Yunus, who is sometimes confused with Yunus Emre. He uses the nickname *Ashik* Yunus (Yunus the Lover) in his poems. He is from Bursa and died in 1439. Some renowned sufi poems which were thought to be Yunus Emre's do indeed belong to this Yunus. "Şol cennetin ırmakları", "Dertli ne ağlayıp gezersin burda", "Sordum sarı çiçeğe", "Adı güzel, kendi güzel Muhammed", "Dertli dolap" are examples of such poems.

General Features of Yunus Emre's Poetry

Yunus Emre uses the language of Oguz Turks of 13th century Anatolia. His literary and linguistic accomplishment played an important role in the development of Old Anatolian Turkish. The words, expressions, metaphors, and the vocabulary he used in his poems was certainly a turning point in Turkish language, establishing it as a sophisticated literary language.

In the time of the Anatolian Seljuk State, Arabic was used as the language of religion and science, and Persian as the language of literature. However, Yunus Emre and some other poets kept using Turkish in their poetry. Although he wrote a considerable number of his poems in *aruz* prosody under the influence of Persian poetry, most of his poems were written in syllabic meter, which is a traditional metric system of

Turkish poetry. Furthermore, all his poems follow rhyme schemes typical to Arabic/Persian and Turkish poetry. However, in an effort to reflect the original meaning, the poems in this book have been translated in free verse, unavoidably causing them to lack some of their original skill and beauty.

The real artistic genius of Yunus Emre is in his use of Turkish in a very groundbreaking way. He contributed much to the formation of Turkish sufi terminology. The language used by Yunus Emre reflects much of the richness of the Islamic-Turkish civilization of his time.

Yunus Emre expressed himself using Turkish vocabulary. However, he also used Arabic and Persian words which were part of the Turkish of his time, and which were easily understood by a general audience. His language was not unfamiliar to ordinary people of that day. His poems contain folk sayings and idioms, Persian and Arabic words adapted into Turkish, along with expressions which reflects the social culture of his time.

Yunus Emre is especially renowned for his expression of deep and perplexing existential truths on the spiritual path to God in an astonishingly simple way.

According to a story circulating among sufi circles, one day Yunus Emre meets Mawlana Jalaluddin Rumi and says to him: "You have made your book, *Masnavi,* very long. If I were you I would just say: *I have been enveloped with flesh and bone / And been seen as Yunus.*"

Sufi Symbolism in Yunus Emre's Poems

The poetry of Yunus Emre is symbolic in character—as with other sufi poems. The main theme of his poetry can easily be discerned as 'Love'.

For sufis, Love is nothing but Divine Love. They express the Journey to God in terms of a lover seeking his beloved, since there is a great similarity between them, except one is carnal and ephemeral and the other, divine and everlasting.

In the beginning of the Journey, the Lover has the bitter consciousness of being separate from the Beloved. This separation is the Affliction the Lover suffers and can only be healed by Union. So, the Affliction is itself the remedy, since Union is only possible through this deep Affliction of the Lover.

This separation causes great grief in the Lover as a consequence of which he cries and wails in desolation, which is but the heartfelt invocation of the Beloved. And, in his arduous journey, the Lover—in his desire for Attainment—risks everything, even his soul.

True Love demands from the Lover that he lose himself, annihilating himself in the Beloved. The existence of the Beloved takes such a crucial importance in the existence of the Lover that nothing remains of him. Also everything loses its value and beauty before the Beloved. This overwhelming Love is symbolized by the moth burning into the candle or a drop merging with the ocean.

Thus through Love, through annihilation of his self or *nafs*, the Lover recognizes the true nature of existence and becomes a Gnostic. He sees the Beloved, God, ever-present in everything through the self-manifestation of His Names and Attributes. There is no way to recognize it without the annihilation of the self, and there can be no way to annihilate the self without Love.

In traditional poems, depicting earthly love, there are terms used metaphorically to symbolize the beauty of the beloved. When such metaphorical terms used in sufi poetry, the symbolism is doubled and takes on a deeper spiritual meaning. For instance, while in traditional poetry, "pearl" is a metaphor for the teeth of the beloved, indicating beauty, in sufi poetry it is used as a metaphor for divine knowledge.

There are a number of his poems where the meaning is very hard to understand, being expressed with a very symbolic language. One of his poems begins with these words:

> *I climbed a plum tree,*
> *There I ate grapes;*
> *The garden owner yelled:*
> *"Why have you eaten my walnuts?"*
>
> *I put mud bricks into a cauldron*
> *And boiled them with the north wind,*
> *To whosoever asked "what is that?"*
> *Into it I dipped and gave its essence.*

This poem, which continues with an apparent 'surrealist' depiction of things which seems to be making fun of us, ends with the words:

> *Yunus has spoken such words*
> *The like of which were never heard;*
> *Attainers to God veil their meaning*
> *From the ignorant.*

This poem has been interpreted by other sufis such as Niyazi-i Misri to reveal its deep hidden meaning. When the poem is read through the interpretation of Niyazi Misri, one realizes that Yunus Emre indeed talks about spiritual truths with this elusive poem. For instance, here, "plum" symbolises *sharia*, "grape" symbolises *tariqa*, "walnut" symbolises *haqiqa*, and "the garden owner" symbolises the spiritual guide.

Here, it should be noted that the poems in his *Divan* were written in different spiritual states. There are poems written both at the early stages of the Way and in later stages too. So, each poem in the Divan reflects the spiritual state of Yunus Emre at the time of writing.

Yunus Emre as a Sufi

It's also astonishing to see that it's so uncertain which *tariqa* Yunus Emre follow since his poetry makes no specific reference to any *tariqa*. We see that different sources depict him as a Bektashi or a Mawlawi or a Qadiri dervish, which all might be true—or false. However, we are not all clueless in this matter. Yunus Emre mentions a name, Tapduk Emre, so respectfully nineteen times in his *Divan* that it is all-evident that Yunus Emre was a dervish under the spiritual guidance of Tapduk Emre, an Anatolian sufi master who lived in central Anatolia, around somewhere between Eskişehir and Ankara. So, we might hope that the name Tapduk Emre may lead us somewhere about Yunus Emre. However, the uncertainty persists, as there is also a great uncertainty concerning which *tariqa* Tapduk Emre followed. However, he is mostly thought to be on the spiritual lineage of Hodja Ahmed Yasawi, through Hadji Bektash Veli.

Another important name Yunus Emre mentions in one of his poems is Mawlana Jalaluddin Rumi, the founder of the Mawlavi *tariqa*. In that poem he reveals his high esteem for him:

Since His Highness Mawlana Rumi
Regarded me,
His mighty regard has been the mirror
Of my heart.

What we can see clearly is that Yunus Emre is highly respected among all Anatolian sufi circles. At the beginning of his *Divan*, the introductory words written by those who compiled the poems into a book may give a clear indication of this:

> *This is the Divan of Yunus Emre,*
> *who is the most beautiful of the poets,*
> *the most fluent of fluent writers,*
> *the Sultan of those who attained to God,*
> *the one who is highly esteemed by the Poor,*
> *the overseer of the Forlorn,*
> *and the leader of the Lovers.*
>
> *May God sanctify his soul.*
> *And, as he let the worlds be benefitted*
> *with his favor and generosity,*
> *may he let us benefit*
> *from his blessing and benevolence.*

Sheikh Suleyman Efendi of Kyustendil (d.1819) in his book *Bahr-ul Velaye*—a collection of biographies of sufi masters—when writing about Yunus Emre, states that: "It is related that Mawlana Jalaluddin Rumi has said: 'To whatever divine waystations I have ascended, there I have found the trace of an old Turkoman, whom I could never surpass.' It was Yunus Emre that he was referring to."

JOURNEY
TO
THE BELOVED

1

Aşkun aldı benden beni
Bana seni gerek seni

Your Love has intoxicated me,
I am in need, in need of You;
I am burning night and day,
I am in need, in need of You.

I neither enjoy bounty
Nor am sorrowful for poverty,
I take comfort only in Your Love,
I am in need, in need of You.

Your Love slays Lovers,
Makes them dive into the Sea of Love,
Fills them with divine manifestations,
I am in need, in need of You.

Let me break the chains of Love,
Let me, love-crazed, to the mountains flee;
Day and night, all I think of is You,
I am in need, in need of You.

If they kill me,
And scatter my ashes to the air,
There, what remains of me will declare:
I am in need, in need of You.

Sufis need discourses delivered by the Guide,
Men of obedience need the hereafter,
Majnuns need their Laila,
I am in need, in need of You.

I have no place in hell,
I have no mansion in paradise,
I have cried a lot for You,
I am in need, in need of You.

What they call Heaven
Is but a house and a few Hooris,
Give it to whosoever wants it so,
I am in need, in need of You.

If Joseph had seen
Your image once in his dream,
He would abandon all his belongings,
I am in need, in need of You.

They call me *Yunus*,
I burn more fiercely each and every day;
I seek You in both worlds,
I am in need, in need of You.

2

İlim ilim bilmekdür ilim kendin bilmekdür
Sen kendüni bilmezsin yâ niçe okumakdur

Knowledge is knowing knowledge,
And knowledge is but knowing oneself;
If you know yourself not,
What use to study those books?

The object of studying is
To know Him;
If you know not what you study,
It is but an empty effort.

Never say: I have studied, I have learnt,
Never say: I have worshipped a lot;
If you do not know the Perfect Man as Truth,
Yours is but a vain pursuit.

The meaning of the Four Books
Is evident in one Alif;
You say: "Alif", O teacher,
But do you know the meaning of it?

Yunus Emre says: O teacher,
Entering a heart
Is better than making Pilgrimage
A thousand times.

3

Gönlüm düşdi bir sevdâya
Gel gör beni aşk n'eyledi

My heart has fallen into such a Love,
Come, see what Love has done to me.
I am wailing with tears,
Come, see what Love has done to me.

I walk in flames,
Love has painted me with blood,
Neither sane nor insane am I,
Come, see what Love has done to me.

I walk here and there,
Asking everywhere for the Friend,
No one knows my state of affairs in these foreign lands,
Come, see what Love has done to me.

My face has grown pale,
My breast torn apart,
O brother, you are heartbroken like me,
Come, see what Love has done to me.

I walk in foreign lands,
Only in dreams the Friend do I see;
Waking up, love-crazed Majnun I become,
Come, see what Love has done to me.

Now I rise like clouds of dust,
Now I blow like the wind,
Now I cascade like water in flood,
Come, see what Love has done to me.

I surge like flowing water,
My wounded breast I tear apart,
I shed tears, remembering my Guide,
Come, see what Love has done to me.

Take my hand, raise me up,
You to join;
You made me cry, now make me laugh,
Come, see what Love has done to me.

I am *Yunus* the destitute,
All covered in wounds,
Wandering in the land of the Friend,
Come, see what Love has done to me.

4

Cânlar cânını buldum bu cânum yağma olsun
Assı ziyândan geçdüm dükkânum yağma olsun

I have found the Soul of souls,
Let my soul be plundered now;
I care not for profit nor for loss,
Let my shop be plundered now.

I have abandoned my self,
Cast aside the veil of the eye;
I have attained my Friend,
Let my doubt be plundered now.

My self has been annihilated,
All my possessions by the Friend are owned;
I have become placeless,
Let my place be plundered now.

I am fed up with duality,
I have worn the garment of Love;
I am replete from the table of Affliction,
Let my remedy be plundered now.

Having given up my existence,
To me the Friend has come to me.
My ruined heart has been filled with Light,
Let my world be plundered now.

I have abandoned unending ambition,
Fed up with the succession of seasons;
I have found the Owner of the Garden,
Let my garden be plundered now.

I have cut all relations,
I have flown towards the Friend;
I have fallen into the Council of Love,
Let my council be plundered now.

O *Yunus*, you utter pleasant words,
Of honey and of sugar you eat;
I have found the honey of honeys,
Let my hive be plundered now.

5

Sana ibret gereğise gel göresin bu sinleri
Ger taşısan eriyesin bakup göricek bunları

If you need a lesson, come see these graves;
Even though you are a stone
You shall be softened
By looking at them.

See those rich people, what happened to them all?
Finally they had to wear
A sleeveless robe
– The shroud.

Now where is he who says "sovereignty is mine"?
Pleased with nothing he was – neither palace nor pavilion;
Now it is only a hut –the grave– where they sleep,
Only a stone –an epitaph– is what survives them.

They cannot enter the house – the heart,
They can neither worship nor devote themselves to God;
They cannot find the prosperity they used to have
For their epoch, their life-times have passed.

Where are the men of sweet words?
Where are the men whose faces shon like the sun?
Now they are lost,
Of them remains no trace.
Once they were lords
With slaves by their doors,
Now you cannot discern
Who is the slave and who is the lord.

No door there is,
No meal to eat,
There is no light to see,
Their daytime has become night.

O *Yunus*, even what you say "is mine"
Will also be taken;
One day,
You, too, will be as them.

6

Gel iy gözüm ağla gülmezem ayruk
Cânum dosta gider gelmezem ayruk

Come, weep, O eyes, I will laugh no more,
My soul goes to the Friend, I will return no more.

What if I die in this world but once,
There will be no more death, I will die no more.

My existence I have transformed into nothingness;
Today, I abide with my self no more.

I have been a diver into the Ocean of Love,
Into the river of Amu Darya I will dive no more.

Your Love reduced me to ashes;
Being saturated by Your Color, I will be blanched no more.

Let me lay on the threshold of the Friend;
It is enough, I will leave there no more.

Let my soul be burnt in the fire of Love;
Let my tears flow, I will wipe them no more.

Let me burn in my heartbreak;
Falling in Love, I will die no more.

To your generosity I plead, do not cast me aside;
O my Guide, what is other than You I will love no more.

Yunus is in Love; he wants his Beloved;
Nothing other than You, no more.

7

Bu yokhk yohna bugün bize yoldaş olan kimdür
İlümüze gönilelüm sorun kardaş olan kimdür

Who is it that, today, accompanies us
On the Path of Annihilation?
When heading to our Homeland,
Who is our brother on the way?

We have stayed so long in this land
With heavy burdens,
Who is it that, sweeping away those afflictions,
And those constructions, becomes like us?

He has sent you here – to this world,
Only going for a stroll;
O scholar, you are building a house,
Who is it that their house is ruined?

Being deceived by this world,
We have yet to reach the Throne;
Who is it that serves both on earth
And on that Throne?

O come, let us go,
Yunus has set off and is headed,
Powerless and helpless,
Who is it that leads on this Path?

8

Bir şâha kul olmak gerek hergiz ma'zûl olmaz ola
Bir eşik yasdanmak gerek kimse elden almaz ola

One has to be the servant of a King
Who can never be overthrown,
One must lay his face upon a threshold
Which can never be ousted.

One has to fly like a bird,
One has to retire to a place of quiet,
One has to drink a sweet syrup
Which ever intoxicates.

One has to be a swift fish,
One has to wander abroad with delight,
One has to smell a rose
Which never pales.

One has to fall in Love,
One has to find the Beloved,
One has to burn with the fire of Love,
Not to be burnt anymore.

A feast must be given,
An honoring must be made,
A word must be uttered,
A word known by none.

One must know God,
One must be informed of Him,
One must die whilst alive,
So he will never die.

O poor *Yunus*, keep calm,
Turn your face towards Him,
Bring a Man like Tapduk,
Unequaled in the world.

9

Biz dünyâdan gider olduk kalanlara selâm olsun
Bizüm içün hayır-duâ kılanlara selâm olsun

We are departing from this world,
Blessings upon those who remain;
Blessings upon those
Who say auspicious prayers for us.

Death leaves us helpless
And deprives us of speech;
Blessings upon those
Who, when we are ill, inquire after us.

There we will lie bare,
Our collarless shrouds will be made;
Blessings upon those
Who wash us with purity for burial.

The Angel of Death takes our soul,
The blood in our veins runs dry;
Blessings upon those
Who lay and wrap us in our shroud.

Our purpose unattained,
We go to the Friend;
Blessings upon those
Who attend our funeral prayer,
Muttering some words about us,
With a grievance in their hearts;
Blessings upon those
Who bring and place us in the grave.

Here, all those who came will leave,
They are upon a way of no return;
Blessings upon those
Who ask after us.

The Lover is one who loves Him,
And God remedies his Affliction;
Blessings upon those
Who say auspicious prayers for us.

Poor *Yunus* utters these words,
His eyes full with tears of blood;
What do the ignorant know?
Blessings upon those who know us.

10

Taşdun yine deli gönül sular gibi çağlar mısın
Akdun yine kanlu yaşum yollarum bağlar mısın

You have overflown, O crazed heart,
Would you cascade like water?
You have poured down, O bloody tears,
Would you waylay my road?

I am helpless, my hands reach not my Beloved,
For my Affliction no remedy is to be found;
I have been away from my homeland,
Would you entertain me here – in these foreign lands?

I have lost my companion,
My breast cannot be healed;
O bloody tears,
Would you, like a river, cascade?

While I have been dust on your road,
You look beyond;
Are you those stone-hearted mountains,
That tower over me?

O snowy mountain, that lies in my way,
I have been kept apart from my Beloved;
Would you, like a bandit,
Obstruct my road?
O clusters of cloud that hang
Atop of the snow-capped mountains,
Would you, loosening your hair,
Weep tears for me?

The soul of *Yunus* is intoxicated,
I am on the road, but where are my lands?
Yunus did see you in a dream,
Wondering how you are – are you ill or well?

11

Yirün göğün safâsı Mustafâ'dur
Kamu ahdün vefâsı Mustafâ'dur

The bliss of the earth and of the heavens, is Mustafa,
The safekeeping of the promise is with Mustafa.

His forehead is a full moon, his eyelashes, a crescent,
The light of day is Mustafa.

The Throne is like the earth, under his feet,
The completion of creation is in Mustafa.

On the Day of Judgement, he will be the Interceder,
The light of the eight Heavens is Mustafa.

To the helpless, disobedient servants
The one who will Intercede is Mustafa.

Tomorrow, when the prophets are powerless,
The one who will hold your hand is Mustafa.

Beseech God, O *Yunus,* and praise Him,
His Friend, His Beloved, is Mustafa.

12

Ben bir aceb ile geldüm kimse hâlüm bilmez benüm
Ben söylerem ben dinlerem kimse dilüm bilmez benüm

I have arrived in a strange land,
Where no one knows my state of affairs;
I speak and listen to my own words,
No one knows my language in this land.

My language is the language of the servant,
My land is the land of the Friend,
I am the nightingale, the Friend my rose,
A rose that never fades.

The Friend called me forth,
He offered me a cup to take,
I took the cup and drank the Wine,
From now on, my heart will not die.

I have nowhere to stop,
In no place do I rest;
To invoke God,
I need no particular place.

Ask me the place where I stand,
I will show it to you if you come;
Other than Him
My eyes do not see even a jot.

See what was made manifest
To Moses on Mount Sinai;
Yunus says: with God
My words do not go unheard.

13

Hak'dan gelen şerbeti içdük el-hamdülillâh
Şol kudret denizini geçdük el-hamdülillâh

We have drunk the sweet Wine bestowed by our Beloved
– Praise be to God;
We have traversed the Sea of Might
– Praise be to God.

We have surmounted distant mountains,
We have passed oak barrens and gardens;
We have passed beyond them all, in health and in happiness
– Praise be to God.

We were dry, now we are fresh,
We were the foot, now we are the head;
We grew wings, now we are birds that soar
– Praise be to God.

To the lands we have visited,
And, to the pure hearts,
We have radiated the meaning of Tapduk
– Praise be to God.

Come here, let us make peace,
If you are stranger, let us be friends;
Our horses being saddled, we rode our way
– Praise be to God.

Down we descended into Anatolia the winter to spend,
There we committed many a good deed and evil so;
Then, with the arrival of spring, back we returned
– Praise be to God.

Being gathered, a spring did we become,
And being gathered more, a river wide;
Flowing, we poured into the sea and overflowed
– Praise be to God.

We are in the presence of Tapduk,
As servants at his door,
O poor *Yunus* once raw, now you are cooked
– Praise be to God.

14

Sen bu cihân mülkini Kâf'tan Kâf'a tutdun tut
Yâ bu âlem mâhm oynayuban ütdün tut

Suppose that you have purchased
All the estates of this world,
Suppose that you have gambled
And have won all the possessions in this world.

Sitting on the throne
In the palace of Solomon,
Suppose that you have been giving orders
To creatures one and all.

Suppose that along with these possessions
You add
The treasure of Feridun,
And that of Nushirewan and of Qarun.

This world is but a morsel
Chewed in the mouth,
Why hold in your mouth what you have chewed?
Suppose it has already been swallowed.

Your life is but a string on a bow,
How can the arrow stay
On the bow already drawn?
Suppose you have already thrown it away.

Suddenly they will call you from this world,
Think that moment is now,
Suppose you already prepared yourself
And have gone.

You have submerged into the sea,
You have begun to drown,
Do not madly thrash about, O helpless one,
Suppose you have already sunken down.

Every breath you take
Diminishes your pouch,
As your pouch is half-empty,
Suppose it has already been spent.

One day you will taste
The syrup of death,
For sure you will taste it,
Suppose it has already been downed.

One day you will die,
You know that death is a truth;
Separating from all,
Suppose you already lie in your grave.

O *Yunus*, what if you live
One hundred pleasant years?
It will end with one last breath,
Suppose it has already been exhaled.

15

Ben derd ile âh iderdüm derdüm bana dermâmmış
İsteridüm hasret ile dost yanumda pinhâmmış

I had been sighing from Affliction,
I found that my affliction was itself my remedy;
I had been longing for the Friend,
I found that He was hidden by my side.

I had been thinking of Him everywhere,
I had been raising my head to the heavens in praise,
I had been longing for the Friend,
I found that He was hidden by my side.

I had been imagining I was separate,
That the Friend and I were apart;
Then I knew that what makes me imagine such
Is this attribute of man.

Whoever knows the Perfect Man,
Leaving behind his animality, becomes a man;
For all creation,
The Perfect Man is a Sultan.

All that there is, is unified,
And Adam it is who knows this unity;
Whosoever this unity denies,
To his very self is an enemy.

Whoever becomes a Man, finds God,
And, delivers Wine
In the gathering of Friends,
Like this poor *Yunus*, intimate with Love.

16

İy âşıkân iy âşıkân aşk mezhebi dîndür bana
Gördi gözüm dost yüzüni yas kamu düğündür bana

Lovers! O Lovers! My religion is but
The sect of Love;
My eyes have seen the Friend's Face,
No more to lament, everything is but a feast.

That which is other than God
Saddens me not,
Nor does it stain my heart,
I only hear the beautiful voice of God.

Let me speak no more of
"I" to myself nor "you" abroad,
Nor the words "servant" and "Sultan",
Their hearers to confound.

My way reaches to You from You,
My tongue tells of You from You,
Yet, my hand cannot reach You,
How is this? – I am all perplexed.

From Your Love, let me stray not
From Your presence, let me not be expulsed
And, as I set off,
May I reach You, through You.

The Friend has sent us
To see the world,
So, I came and see, what an ornament it is,
Yet, if one loves You, it is cast aside.

He promised to his servants:
Tomorrow you will see Me;
I do not have to wait for that blessed day –
Him, here and now, I do see.

Having fallen in Love,
The world and the hereafter are one;
To me past and eternity
Are like yesterday and today.

Yunus has rendered unto You
His religion and his faith;
What is today and what is tomorrow
When you are in Love?

17

Ger vuslata erdünise bu derd ile firâk nedür
Dost yakîn gördünise bu bakduğun ırak nedür

If you have joined the Beloved,
What is this affliction and separation?
If you have seen the Friend up close,
Why do you look far away?

The very existence of the Man of Union
Should be annihilated;
To enter into this Path, let us see,
How can one prepare oneself?

If you are a Man of Union,
If you have known the veil of the eyes,
If you have seen the Friend manifestly,
What is the use of this existence? Cast it aside!

Knowledge is but a veil over the eyes,
It arranges finances for this world and for the hereafter;
The real Book is the Book of Love,
So, what use are those pages you read?

Take heed and open your eyes,
Your very self is the trap you should recognize;
Pass to the abode of the Friend
– The ultimate station.

Your eyes can see,
They transform the words into meaning;
Is the candle burning at night the same
When compared to the Sun?

Yunus says: Openly and in secret,
Of God the two worlds are not empty;
If what you seek is the Friend,
What Hoori, what Mansion, what Buraq?

18

Çıkdum erik dahna anda yidüm üzümi
Bostân ıssı kakıyup dir ne yirsin kozum

I climbed a plum tree,
There I ate grapes;
The garden owner yelled:
"Why have you eaten my walnuts?"

I put mud bricks into a cauldron
And boiled them with the north wind,
To whosoever asked "what is that?"
Into it I dipped and gave its essence.

I gave yarn to the cloth-maker,
But he did not make a ball of string;
Yet he calls me:
"Come quickly, your cloth is ready".

I loaded a wing of a sparrow onto forty ox carts,
Yet, even twice more could not have carried it,
Thus, was it stranded
In the fields.

A fly shook and brought an eagle to the ground,
No lie is this;
It really did happen,
I also saw its traces in the dust.

A fish climbed a tree
To eat some pickled tar;
The white stork gave birth to a foal,
Never cease such wonders!

I wrestled with an armless wrestler,
He grabbed my feet with no hands,
I could not beat him,
He hurt me very badly.

They threw me a stone
From Mount Qaf;
As it was dropped half way,
My face barely escaped being hurt badly!

I whispered to a blind man,
A deaf person did hear,
A mute man utters
The words on my tongue.

I slayed an ox
And laid it on the ground,
The owner of the ox appeared and yelled:
"You have slayed my goose!"

I commit a theft on another's behalf,
And he slandered me;
A seller came and said:
"What have you done with my mirror?"

I stopped by a turtle,
A mole was his companion,
I asked: "Where are you travelling?"
He heads for Kayseri.

Yunus has spoken such words
The like of which were never heard;
Attainers to God veil their meaning
From the ignorant.

19

Benüm bunda karârum yok ben bunda gitmeğe geldüm
Bezirgânam metâm çok alana satmağa geldüm

I will not rest here, I came here to leave,
I am a merchant, with many goods,
I came to sell
To any purchaser.

I have not come for selfish assertions,
My task is Love;
The heart is the Friend's abode,
And I have come to build hearts.

I am mad with Love,
Only Lovers know what is my state of affairs;
Altering my duality,
Unity to attain.

He is my Guide, I his servant,
The nightingale of the Friend's garden;
In the garden of my Guide,
I have come to sing cheerfully.

The souls who do not make acquaintance here,
Will make no acquaintance there;
Making acquaintance with the Friend here,
I have come to humbly declare my state of affairs.

Yunus Emre has fallen in Love,
And has died with the Affliction of the Beloved;
I have come to humbly declare my state of affairs
At the door of the true Man of God.

20

Anca zâr eyleyen kim şol bülbül eyler
Am ol eylemez illâ gül eyler

Who is that crying? It is the nightingale!
That rose it is that makes him cry so.

Upon seeing the Beautiful Face of the Friend,
One yells: It is You who drives me mad with Love!

What does the helpless nightingale see in the rose?
Why does he sing before the rose garden?

What did Majnun behold in the face of Laila,
That he shed endless tears so?

What was revealed to Farhad's eyes,
That to the Friend he forged a road?

What was revealed to Sheikh Ibrahim,
That he cast away his crown and his throne?

He makes one a denier and the other believe,
It is no one but Him that makes them so.

To one afflicted He never makes him sigh,
To another He makes his afflictions thrive.

Never say: that is rich and this is poor,
Be it rich, be it poor, He makes them so.

To one He gives no cloth to cover his all,
To another He covers his horse in a satin pure.

In this world He makes one a beast,
And another His devotee.

He holds that person's hand and raises them to the Throne,
Another He turns to ash and casts them down.

Hide poor *Yunus'* words of gold from fools,
Lest they turn them into nothing but worthless copper.

21

İy pâdişâh-ı Lem-yezel kıldum yönüm senden yana
İş bu yüzüm karasıyla vasl isterem senden yana

O Eternal Sultan!
I have turned towards You;
Shameful of myself,
I yearn to reach You.

You are the One who sees through my eyes,
You are the One who speaks with my tongue,
You are the One who brought me to life,
From beginning to end, You are the One.

You said to me O Lord:
I am closer to you than your very self.
Since You are closer than me,
Show me Your Beautiful Face!

You are close to me, yet I yearn for You,
Though I search day and night,
I cannot see You,
And so I am perplexed!

He is all that comes and He is all that goes,
He is the One who is seen,
He is the One who sees,
He is the lowly and the sublime.

O *Yunus*, this is the secret of God,
And it is inexpressible;
Known only through tasting,
And not through the mind.

22

Benem sâhib-kırân devrân benümdür
Benem key pehlevân meydân benümdür

I am the overpowering king,
The reign is mine,
I am the mighty wrestler,
The arena is mine.

I have no fear
Of any waylayer,
This God-given power and strength
Is mine.

Abu Bakr and Omar,
Ali and Uthman,
–Those venerable men of religion–
All are mine.

Let the one who is poor come to me
To become rich;
This property, this capital,
This shop, all are mine.

Hasan is the light of faith
In my body,
Huseyn, the Man of Knowledge,
He is mine.

I am *Yunus* in this world,
I am the servant
Of the Sultan,
And, that Sultan is mine.

23

Cânm aşk yohna virmeyen âşık mıdur
Cehd eyleyüp ol dosta irmeyen âşık mıdur

One who does not sacrifice his soul for the sake of Love
– Is he a Lover?
One who does not struggle to reach the Friend
– Is he a Lover?

One who does not sip from the Cup of Love,
One who does not abandon the desires of the self,
One who does not stand like a Man on the way to God
– Is he a Lover?

One who does not wholeheartedly strengthen
The Love of the Friend,
One who does not close the roll of worldly aspirations
– Is he a Lover?

One who is not always in abstention,
One who does not observe retreat,
One who does not see any trace of the Face of the Beloved
– Is he a Lover?

In Love, there is no room for mere acquaintanceship,
And not every soul can ascend to Heaven;
One who does not burn in the fire like a moth
– Is he a Lover?

When one is stricken with Love's Affliction
He demands the remedy,
One who does not seek the remedy for his Affliction
– Is he a Lover?

O *Yunus*,
Endure the cruelties of your Friend,
One whose heart is not wounded with the arrow of Love
– Is he a Lover?

24

Hakîkatün ma'nîsin şerh ile bilmediler
Erenler bu dirliği riyâ dirilmediler

They have not known the meaning of Truth
Through commentaries,
The Friends of God are enlivened
Without hypocrisy.

The Truth is a sea
Upon which Sharia is a ship,
Yet many, not leaving the ship,
Have not dived into the sea.

The Sharia fellows pursue
Selfish assertions,
But Attainers to Reality
Leave them behind.

One who explains the Four Books
Is but a denier of Truth,
For while reading the exegesis,
They could not grasp the meaning.

O *Yunus*, if you follow this Way,
You will be named 'faithful';
But those yet to change their names
Have not set off on the Way.

25

İy sözlerün ashn bilen gel di bu söz kandan gelür
Söz ashm anlamayan sanur bu söz benden gelür

O you who know the origin of words,
Tell me, from where does this word emerge?
One who does not know the truth
Surmises that, from me this word emerges.

Some words lift the heart,
Some words do friendships break apart;
Be it contemptible, be it honorable,
Everything with a word does start.

The word is not from ink and paper,
Not from what is written nor read,
That word comes – not from walking creatures,
But from the voice of the Creator.

I have not read the letters of the alphabet,
My speech is not of this world;
Even one hundred thousand fortune-tellers do not know
From which star my fortune flows.

The light shining upon us emanates not from the Moon,
The Man of Love has nothing to do with words;
Not from that house do we receive our lot,
From a vast ocean does it spring.

In the beginning, God wrote a script
Upon the tablet of the heart;
It originates from pre-eternity
The lesson that is studied now.

First, He addresses the soul,
Then to this body the soul does come,
Mere tools we are,
Nothing more.

My intelligence looks to that tablet
And discloses my secret Afflictions;
A word appears and flows to my heart,
A word springs suddenly to the tongue.

We are just a pretext in between,
We are helpless, we can be nothing more;
As God orders the soul,
So this speech ensues from there.

O *Yunus*, sighs because of this Affliction,
Comfort has no room in trouble's abode;
The remedy to this Affliction comes
When sighs with sighs are burned.

26

İki cihan zindâmsa gerek bana bostân ola
Ayruk bana ne gam gussa çün inâyet dosttan ola

If the two worlds are a prison,
Let them be but a fragrant garden to me;
No more sorrow and anxiety,
As the Friend does bless me.

Let me reach the Friend, be His servant,
Let me be an ever-blooming rose,
Let me sing, be a nightingale,
The rose garden my abode.

My eyes have seen the Friend,
And, I am a servant of His friends;
For those who understand,
My words are sweet sugar.

Without You, these two worlds
To me are but a prison;
One who tastes Your Love,
Abides with the Purest of the Pure.

One who abandons all selfish assertions,
One who aspires to none but God,
One who drinks the Wine of Love
– Becomes drunk.

The hypocrites are blind,
And tomorrow shall be shamed;
The bitter words of folk,
Should taste as sweet as sugar.

Let me always praise God,
Laying my face to the ground;
Let me devote my self to the Friend,
Selfish assertions – no more.

As I succumbed to Love,
My inner secret itself revealed;
O *Yunus,* may these words of yours be heard
Across the worlds.

27

Sensüz yola girürisem çârem yok adım atmağa
Gövdemde kuvvetüm sensin başum götürüp gitmeğe

If I set off on my way without You,
I cannot take a step;
You are the power of my body,
That lets me wend my way.

My heart, my soul, my mind, my knowledge
Only find rest with You;
They never stop soaring
To reach You, O Friend.

Whosoever abandons himself,
His Beloved will make of him a hawk
And set him upon flocks of ducks and partridges
To capture them.

Can he be called a Lover
Who aspires to Heaven?
Even It is but a trap,
Ensnaring a believer's soul.

God gives the Lover
The strength of a thousand Hamzas;
Thus he dislodges mountains,
Forging his way to the Friend.

A hundred thousand Ferhads
Hew the mountains;
Cutting away the rock,
They let the Water of Life flow.

The fountain of the Water of Life
Is where Lovers join their Beloved;
And the full cups the Beloved serves
Burn the parched.

The Lover should be all empty
And be surrendered on the Way;
He lowers his head to whatever anyone does,
As he cannot break anyone's heart.

The sigh of Lovers
Burns away the seven Hells,
Merging the eight Heavens
Into Light.

We knew that all those who came have gone,
We saw that all those dwellers have passed away,
But, those souls that drink the Wine of Love
Never die.

The soul of *Yunus* has not been trapped
And has left behind both Heaven and Hell;
Advancing on the Way, only to the Friend he goes
His very Essence to attain.

28

Hak bir gönül virdi bana hâ dimeden hayrân olur
Bir dem gelür şâdî olur bir dem gelür giryân olur

God has given me a soul,
Bewildered wheresoever it casts its glance;
Now in bliss,
Now in tears.

Now like winter,
The coldest time of year has come;
And then, from glad tidings, is born
And springs, a pleasant garden.

Now it keeps silent,
Expounding not a word;
Then pearls, spreading from its mouth,
Heal wounded hearts.

Now my soul ascends to the Throne,
Now it descends beneath the earth;
Now one may think it is but a drop,
Now it overflows and becomes an ocean.

Now it remains in ignorance,
Oblivious to all;
Now, diving deep into wisdom,
Becomes Galen and becomes Luqman.

Now it becomes a giant or a nymph,
Desolate places its only abode;
Now, soaring with the Queen of Sheba,
It becomes Solomon, the sultan of all.

Now becoming a beggar,
Shoddy rags barely covering my all;
Then thanks to His abundant favour,
An emperor raised tall.

Now becoming disobedient
And heedless;
Now faith and piety
Are my companions.

Now transfixed with sin,
On the road to Hell straight;
Now seeing His compassion, becoming Ridvan,
The Guardian of Heaven's gate.

Now frequenting mosques,
It lays its face to the ground;
Now reading the Bible and becoming clergy,
In the church it may be found.

Now becoming Moses,
One hundred thousand times in invocation;
Then, becoming Pharaoh and Haman,
It resides in the abode of arrogance.

Now it revives the dead
Like Jesus;
Then, losing its way,
It walks abroad in confusion.

Now it becomes Gabriel,
Spreading benediction everywhere,
Now it loses its way
– So bewildered, poor *Yunus* it becomes.

29

Sensin bize bizden yakın görünmezsin hicâb nedür
Çün aybı yok görklü yüzün üzerinde nikâb nedür

Closer than our very selves, still You are not seen,
What makes You hidden so?
Since your Beautiful Face is without flaw,
Then why is It veiled?

You said, O Sultan,
That You "guide whosoever You wish";
No one has power against You, O Sovereign,
So, who then is guilty, why this torment?

Who writes on the Tablet?
Who is astray and who is misled?
Who designs all these tasks?
What is the answer to these questions?

Your Name is Compassionate,
Your Mercy You have proclaimed,
The Guides have heralded: "Do not abandon hope"
– What is that addressing?

All tasks are Yours,
It is You who give and take back;
While You do whatever You wish,
What then is the questioning in the hereafter?

We seek Your Generosity
As all things come out as You wish;
What then is this handful of dust
From Your Compassion?

Saying "Be!" You have created
What there is;
Why would You destroy it
Then with another word?

Where is the Sultan of this reign?
You are the flesh, but where is its soul?
Those eyes wish to see Him
Then where is that place of return?

O *Yunus*, these eyes cannot see Him,
Those who see Him speak not;
This way-station –the world– is incomprehensible,
What is this mirage that You have brought forth?

30

Âşıklar ortasında sofîlik satmayalar
İhlâs ile bu aşka riyâyı katmayalar

Among the Lovers
Do not pretend to be a sufi;
Do not stain sincerity and Love
With hypocrisy.

Either say what you know
Or listen from one who does;
Hold tight the rope of submission,
Lengthen not your words.

He said: the Koran is My Words,
And the heart My House;
If one knows not the owner of his heart,
As a human being regard him not.

Sharia is waxed honey,
Purified butter, the Tariqa;
For the Friend's sake,
Blend the honey into the butter.

The Man of Knowledge relinquishes his life, cares not,
But the liar cannot sacrifice
Even his possessions
– Truth and lie cannot be regarded as one.

Know the esteem of this Breath;
The inner reality of the Attainers
Is not sold to one
With no intent to acquire.

Adam was mistaken;
He ate the wheat in Heaven;
If you know this as His will,
You do not blame Satan.

Do pleasant deeds, say sweet words;
In Sohbet,
Let *Yunus*
Always be remembered.

31

İşidün iy ulular âhir zamân ohsar
Sağ müsülmân seyrekdür ol da gümân ohsar

O men of esteem, listen,
The end of days is upon us now,
True Muslims will be rare,
And there will be widespread doubt.

The scholar will not heed what he reads,
The dervish will not set his sights on the Way,
People will not take admonitions,
What a troubled time it will be!

The generosity of rulers will depart,
They will ride aloof upon their horses;
They will fleece the poor
And be ferocious toward them.

The Man of God
From iniquity has himself withdrawn;
When Dajjal appears,
The end of days will surely come.

He who thinks on the evil of others,
Surmises his own evildoings will not return;
Tomorrow, on the Day of Judgement,
All his deeds will be made known.

O *Yunus*, spend your days
In Love,
The One you love
Will be the Soul of your soul.

32

Evliyâya münkirler Hak yohna âsidür
Ol yola âsi olan gönüllerin pâsıdur

Those who deny the Friends of God
Are disobedient on His Way;
And that which is disobedient
Is but tarnish on the heart.

I suffered the torment of Love
Till the Beloved I did join;
Since, for my Affliction,
That Friend is the sole remedy.

Before the earth came to be,
Before the heavens were formed;
The homeland of the Friends of God
Was the castle of the Sultan.

Since His Highness Mevlana Rumi
Regarded me,
His mighty regard has been the mirror
Of my heart.

Forsake everything for the Beloved
Cleanse yourself of arrogance and of hate;
This world is but ephemeral,
With no one does it remain.

When Geyikli Hasan speaks,
It is the Tongue of Might
Which utters
– Those words are not his own.

Without reading and without writing,
Without doing wrong and going astray,
Yunus knows those who understand
These words of Love.

33

Keleci bilen kişinün yüzini ağ ide bir söz
Sözi pişürüp diyenün işini sağ ide bir söz

A word honors the one
Who knows how to talk,
A word purifies the deeds of one
Who weighs his words before he speaks.

There is a word which halts war,
There is a word which cultivates crops,
There is a word which makes the poisonous meal
Honey and butter.

Weigh your words before you speak,
The worthless to eschew;
Filtering your words with reason,
Utter no word childishly.

Come, O brother, listen to my words,
There is a word which can make
A heap of golden coins and pearls
Dark soil.

Let one know the right time to speak,
Let him not say bad words;
There is a word which can turn this hell,
That is, the world, into eight Heavens.

Walk on your path,
Do not be heedless of what you know;
Be wary of your tongue,
There is a word to wound your soul.

O *Yunus*, watch your words,
There is a word to dismiss you
From the blessed presence
Of your Guide.

34

Bu dünyânun meseli bir ulu şâra benzer
Velî bizüm ömrümüz bir tîz bâzâra benzer

This world is analogous
To a grand city,
Our lifetime is but a street market
That will close very soon.

Whoever comes to this city
Abides here but for a short stay;
He is on a journey
From which there is no turning back.

In the beginning, the taste of this city
Is sweeter than sugar and of honey;
In the end, it is full of pain
Like snake's poison.

In the beginning, it captures the heart
Like a sweetheart;
In the end, it shuns
Like a deceiving hag.

This city is full
Of all manner of delusions,
Deceiving the oblivious
Like a duplicitous witch.

In this deceitful city,
The deluded wander
Like cattle
Amongst the grasses.

From this city, three roads depart,
One leads to Heaven, one to Hell;
And, the third leads
To the Beauty of the Beloved.

This city has a Sultan
Who bestows upon everyone;
One who is intimate with Him
Is truly enlivened.

He who knows his own value,
Knows his own state,
And with Love,
Like spring becomes.

See poor *Yunus*
With Love is crazed;
His each and every breath
Like honey and sugar tastes.

35

Dost senün aşkun okı key katı taşdan geçer
Aşkuna düşen âşık cân ile başdan geçer

O Friend, the arrow of Your Love
Passes through the hardest stone;
The Lover who has fallen in Love with You
Abandons both his body and his soul.

Your Lover's heart
In fire does burn,
Devoting himself to You,
He surrenders his all.

He weeps night and day
And becomes a beloved for Your Love;
As he thinks only of You;
No more turmoil in himself.

For those of Knowledge,
This world is a delusion and a dream;
One who devotes himself to You
Forgoes all.

The love of the world
Is like a poisonous meal,
One who thinks on its very end
Eschews that poisonous meal.

A wise man
Does not do deeds for the hereafter;
Abandoning the beauty of eyes and of eyelashes,
He is not distracted by Hooris.

A real Lover
Hastens to sacrifice his soul;
For the Friend, he gives up his being
Time and time over.

The heart and eyes of *Yunus*
Are full of the Love of God;
One who wishes to hear about the Beloved
Gives up everything and all others.

36

Allah diyelüm dâ'im
Allah görelüm neyler

Let's always recite His name: Allah,
Let's see what Allah does;
Let's stay on the Way,
Let's see what Allah does.

Shed tears saying: Allah,
The very existence of all things He is;
Let's seek Friendship from Him,
Let's see what Allah does.

Let our tongues never forget Him
Let's not forsake that Beloved,
Let's not stray from the Way,
Let's see what Allah does.

The end of hunger is repletion,
The end of repletion is want;
These paths are fearsome,
Let's see what Allah does.

When you least expect it,
Suddenly the veil is removed;
The remedy sweeps away the Affliction,
Let's see what Allah does.

Let's fast in the daytime
Let's keep a vigil of night prayer,
Let's always recite his name: Allah,
Let's see what Allah does.

His name is on tongues,
His Love is in hearts;
On those frightful roads
Let's see what Allah does.

I forsook both name and reputation,
I threw my denial to the water,
I became a Man of Poverty,
Let's see what Allah does.

Let's forever dive into the Ocean,
Let's not be deceived by this world,
Let's be patient with our troubles,
Let's see what Allah does.

I abandoned my shame and honor,
I threw my ashes to the water,
And have become a dervish,
Let's see what Allah does.

O *Yunus,* never surmise that
This Love emanates from you;
He is the Soul of all,
Let's see what Allah does.

What has *Yunus* done, what has he done?
Into a Straight Path has he gone;
He has followed the Men of Guidance,
Let's see what Allah does.

37

Benem ol aşk bahřisi denizler hayrân bana
Deryâ benüm katremdür zerreler ummân bana

I am the fish of the Ocean of Love,
Upon which all the seas marvel;
For me, the ocean is just a drop,
And to me, its drops are but an ocean.

Mount Qaf is not even a speck of mine,
The Sun and Moon are both my servants;
My very essence is God, no doubt,
And my guide, the Koran.

My way leads to the Friend,
My homeland, the world of eternity;
This tongue is of God,
To me, it is neither of servant, nor of sultan.

All that there is was only the Sultan,
Before all was created;
And since I have fallen in Love with the Beloved,
That wound of Love is my only remedy.

Before Adam was created,
Before the soul entered the body,
Before Satan was cursed,
To me, a pavilion was His Throne.

He wanted to see His Face,
He wanted to hear His words,
Giving a glance in one instance,
To me He gave a soul.

Mustafa has been created,
His face is light and his heart is bliss,
He has been faithful to God,
It is he who bestows upon me.

That Precious One was born,
From him emerged all that exists;
Adam, Abraham and Moses
All are evidence to me.

One who is ignorant of the language of Love
Is either insane or a denier;
I know the language of birds,
Which Solomon upon me has conferred .

On this Path, *Yunus Emre* acknowledges his flaws;
Drunkenly he shouts:
How can I be called a dervish?
Such slander it is!

38

Miskîn âdem oğlam nefse zebun olmışdur
Hayvân cânâvâr gibi otlamağa kalmışdur

The piteous son of Adam
Against his own self is weak;
He, like a beast,
Grazes on.

He never thinks of his death,
He never remembers the day he will die,
He is never fed up with this world,
Heedlessness fills his mind.

Fellows do not take admonition,
Gallants do not repent,
Elders do not obey God
– What a troubling time is this!

The rich are astray,
They disregard the poor;
Having left the pool of mercy,
They sink into the self's mire.

These words of *Yunus* are from learned men:
Never be cruel, and always fear death,
For, everyone who is born
One day, will die.

39

Yâr yüreğüm yâr gör ki neler var
Bu halk içinde bize güler var

Cleave, cleave my heart,
See what there is inside;
Amongst people,
Someone ever laughs at us.

Let them laugh,
Since God is with us;
How would the heedless know
There are those who love God?

This way is long,
It has many way-stations,
And there are impassable,
Deep waters on its path.

We have set off on this way
With Love;
We are travelling
To a foreign land.

If you are brave,
Come to the Arena of Love;
Give up your soul,
If you are but able.

There are intoxicated Lovers
Whose eyes shed tear after tear,
Whose breasts are burnt,
All in bewilderment.

O *Yunus,*
Do not aspire to enter
The Arena of Love
– That is solely for the brave.

40

Ol âlem fahri Muhammed nebîler serveridür
Vir salâvât aşk ile ol günâhlar eridür

Muhammad, the Praise of the Universe,
Is the leader of all the prophets;
Praise him with Love,
That praise dissolves sin.

God has praised and created him,
He loved him and called him His beloved;
Mustafa's sweat is
But all the blossoms of this earth.

When Gabriel invited Muhammad
To the Ascension,
In his Ascension, all he wished
Was but his Community.

Be among his Community,
He will not leave you destitute;
Whosoever is from among it,
The eight Heavens are his abode.

Whosoever follows
His Sunnah and his Fard,
He will not be questioned
In the hereafter.

The guilty, the innocent,
All seek his Intercession;
What burns in Hell
Is but the denier's denial.

This *Yunus Emre* has spoken
From his very soul;
The secret to what poor *Yunus* does voice,
Is Tapduk Emre himself.

41

Dervîş olan kişiler deli olagan olur
Aşk neydüğin bilmeyen ana gülegen olur

The dervish is crazed,
Mocked by those incognizant of Love.

But, never laugh at him, it will bring you no good;
For whatever you laugh at, will on you be redoubled.

When one falls in Love, let him endure its Afflictions,
Or else, will he be stranded on this Path.

Becoming a Lover, when one dives
Into the Ocean of Love, pearls will he find.

The Lover has no abode, he abandons the world;
Once it is forsaken, the Beloved is found.

O *Yunus*, neither should you hurt dervishes,
For it is their prayers that are accepted.

42

Bize dîdâr gerek dünyâ gerekmez
Bize ma'nî gerek da'vâ gerekmez

We are in need of the Beloved,
Not of this world;
We are in need of inner truth,
Not of selfish assertions.

For us this is the Night of Power,
Let the dawn not break;
We have no need
Of the morning.

Deliver to us the Wine of Love
O Cupbearer,
We have no need
Of Kauser in Heaven.

The cups are full,
Let's drink them all;
We have no need for wine,
We do not get drunk.

If I fall ill from this Affliction,
No remedy do I want,
I have no need
Of healing.

O Beloved,
My soul is not what I need;
I have no need for anything other
Than Your Beautiful Face.

Yunus, getting drunk,
Has become miserable, the cup in hand;
He gives up his embarrassment,
And invokes his beloved Tapduk.

43

Niçeler bu dünyede günâhın yuyamaz
Ömri geçer yok yire iy dirîğa duyamaz

Many are those
Who cannot purify their sins in this world,
Their lives pass in vain
But, alas, they do not know.

Many are those
That heedlessness has made blind;
Even for His sake, they will not spare
A slice of bread.

This world is a bride,
Embellished in green and in red;
One cannot take his eyes
Off his newlywed.

Death trounces
Many a lion-hearted man,
Unable to resist
Azrael's mighty hand.

Now poor *Yunus* divest all
And set off on Your way;
He with nothing cannot be robbed,
Even by a thousand brigands.

44

Rızık içün gussa yime kimse rızkın kimse yimez
Rızık içün gussa yime pâdişâh eksük eylemez

Do not be troubled by your lot,
No one can take what has been apportioned to you,
Do not be anxious of your provision,
The Sovereign is never deficient.

If you want to take counsel from me,
Let me say from what I know:
Obeying God's order,
Observe the fast and the prayer.

Saying "I observe prayer",
Should you deny the dervishes;
Even if you pray for a thousand years,
You will not be granted pardon.

The prayers the sons of Adam observe
Are not in vain;
That Sovereign never deprives anyone
From His Presence.

Do not carry bad words
From one to another,
We have heard from the noble:
Backbiters are lower than swine.

Yunus says:
I am the servant of the dervishes;
There can be no one in this world
Who does not serve the Sultan.

45

Ben dervîşem diyen kişi iş bu yola âr gerekmez
Derviş olan kişilerün gönli gendür dar gerekmez

O you who call yourself a dervish,
In this Path, abandon shame;
The heart of the dervish is vast,
Never confined.

The dervish has no desire,
He is speechless against the reviler,
Handless against the beater,
And from the heedless apart.

His deeds do not resemble the deeds of ordinary folk,
He drives out confusion from his heart;
A hundred thousand dervishes are but one,
No stranger amongst them.

If you are a dervish,
Everyone is your acquaintance;
Give up useless things,
In between, let there be no other.

Nothingness
Is the treasure of the dervish;
Other than nothingness,
He needs no goods nor possessions.

If you have entered the Way,
And given your heart to a Friend of God,
If you have come with acceptance,
In you, there is no denial.

O *Yunus*, as you have seen the Perfect Man,
Do not multiply the One you see;
Never say: this and that,
A dervish sees beyond multiplicity.

46

Evvel benem âhir benem cânlara cân olan benem
Azup yolda kalanlara hâzır meded iden benem

I am the First, I am the Last,
I am the Soul of souls;
I help those who go astray,
Those who have lost their way.

I am resolved to a decision strictly,
My secret no one hears;
The ignorant know not,
It is me that enters all hearts.

I was a witness at the moment of Creation
And ordered the world in one glance;
It is me who furnishes this inn –the world– with power,
It is me who establishes a foundation for Love.

I have furnished the earth flat,
Upon it mountains to nail,
I wandered the heavens,
And it is me who returns and rests.

I have been the affirmation, religion and faith
For the Lovers;
And I am the denial and Islam,
And the doubt, I am.

To many a people I gave orders,
So, they may live in prosperity;
I am the burning coal, the heated iron,
It is me who beats the anvil, hammer in hand.

It is me who makes snow and freezing ice,
It is me who furnishes animals with subsistence,
Know that, I am the Merciful and the Compassionate
For creatures one and all.

It is me who establishes order in creation,
It is me who wrote the Four Books true,
It is me who writes on blank paper,
I am that written Koran.

I am the one who has joined the Friend,
I am the one whose orders are performed;
I am that gardener
This world to order and to ornament.

I am Rostam the hero,
I am a fragrant garden in the world;
You are the One in front of me,
It is me who sees You through You.

I am the mighty hand of God,
I am Love's nightingale;
Speaking every language,
It is me who informs one and all.

I am the one who loosens the tongues,
I am the one who boils the cauldron of Love,
I am that poisonous black snake
Who let Hamza climb Mount Qaf.

I am the rain that falls to the earth,
I am the cloud that rises to the sky;
I am the murky cloud
Over the eyes of the blind.

It is not *Yunus* who speaks thus,
It is Himself who proclaims;
One who denies, an unbeliever becomes
– I am the First. I am the Last.

47

Yâ ilâhî ger su'âl etsen bana
Bu durur anda cevâbum uş sana

O God, if You are to question me,
This would be my reply:

I have done wrong only to myself,
What have I done to You, O King?

You said: "You are evil" – before my arrival,
You said: "Disobedient Adam" – before my birth.

You cast me as disobedient in pre-eternity,
And, did so proclaim throughout the universe.

You have done whatever You want with me,
Wheresoever I turn, You have turned me.

I have not designed myself, it is You who have designed me so.
Why have You created me as pure shame, O You the All-Rich?

Opening my eyes, all I see is the inside of a dungeon:
The self and whims, all full of Satan.

In this prison, not to die of starvation,
I have eaten things here and there, be they dirty, be they clean.

Has anything diminished from Your possessions?
Have any of my words surpassed Your judgement?

Taking Your provision, have I made You needy?
Or eating Your meal, have I made You hungry?

You make a bridge –thin, like a hair– for me to cross,
That I may drink the Wine of Kauser, having crossed it.

How may Adam pass a bridge as thin as a hair?
Either he falls down or grasps for something or takes to the air.

It is Your generosity which let's him pass
And, upon passing, let's him drink the Wine of Kauser.

Your servants make bridges for good purpose,
The good purpose being that people may get across.

It needs to be strong
So those who see it may say: "This is the right way!"

You have devised a Scale, my sins to weigh,
Intending to cast me into the fire.

The scale is necessary for a shopkeeper,
Or a merchant, or a seller of medicinal herbs.

Sin is the worst of all;
In Your Presence, it is the deed of the evil.

Why do You, revealing it, weigh it so?
Why not cover it with Your favour instead?

You say: "Now I will throw you into the fire
If your evil deeds are heavier."

The evil should be decreased, the good multiplied;
Those who have no good, there, they will perish.

You are the Seer, You know my inner state,
So, why do You need my deeds to weigh?

It could not come to pass, O Lord,
That I would burn in the fire, while You watch.

Isn't your revenge vanquished by putting me to death,
Causing my decay and filling my eyes with dust?

Why so much ado over a handful of earth,
O Generous Lord of Majesty?

Enough! As white hairs do among black grow,
Worldly desires I should abandon.

From *Yunus* no harm has reached You;
You know that which is hidden and that which is manifest.

Let there be no other answer from us to You.
This is all I say: God knows best.

48

İşidün iy yârenler aşk bir güneşe benzer
Aşkı olmayan gönül meseli taşa benzer

Listen, O friends,
Love is like a sun,
And without Love, a heart
Is like stone.

Nothing grows in a heart of stone,
Only poison flows from its tongue;
No matter how soft it speaks,
Its words are like war.

If there is Love, the heart lights up
Softening like a candle;
But blackened stone-hearts
Are like a troubling, hard winter.

At the door of that Sultan,
And before His presence,
The star of Lovers,
Like Venus, forever shines.

Whosoever is full of greed
In his very self is confined;
A cruel companion for himself
– He becomes his own enemy.

Love is a mighty pair of bellows,
Forging the Lovers;
Passing from cup to cup,
They become like silver.

The heart of the Lover never stands still
Until finding his Beloved;
Restless in this world,
Like a bird it flutters.

The denier speaks not the truth,
His words lead nowhere,
Resembling nothing
But incomprehensible illusion.

O *Yunus*, cast aside your anxious thoughts,
Know they are of no use,
What a man needs is Love
To be a dervish.

49

Aşk îmâmdur bize gönül cemâ'at
Kıblemüz dost yüzi dâimdür salât

Love is our Imam,
The heart is Jamaah,
Our Qiblah is the Face of the Friend,
– A perpetual Salah.

The soul prostrates
Before the Mihrab of the Friend
Laying his face down,
He invokes.

As the five times of Salah
Have been unified into one,
How can one observe obedience,
Having been divided into five?

Sharia says:
Keep your promise.
Promises are for those
Who betray.

Seeing the Face of the Friend,
Associating partners is over,
That is why Sharia is left behind
At the doorway.

Nothing compares
To the time of Invoking,
As it is the time of seclusion
With the Friend.

We never oppose
Anyone's religion;
When religion is perfected,
There springs Love.

Our bliss is the Breath
Of the Attainers to God;
That is how we are saved
From mischief.

We said: "Qalu Bala"
In a previous time;
That time is today,
It is this hour.

One who seeks truth
At the door of the Friend,
Finds divine bliss,
Untainted with doubt.

Yunus is imprisoned at that door
In such a way that
He wishes never to be
In comfort.

50

Dîn ü millet soransan âşıklara dîn ne hâcet
Âşık kişi harâb olur âşık bilmez dîn diyânet

If you ask about the religion of Lovers,
Religion is not what they need;
One who is in Love is devastated,
He does not know. What is religion? What is piety?

The heart of the Lover
Always seeks the Beloved;
Being stripped of outward form,
Is it possible for him to be observant?

Obedience leads to Heaven,
And disobedience to Hell;
But the Lover
Is finished with both of them.

One who loves the Friend
Him should he ever seek;
And when with Him he is busied,
Of all else he will be freed.

From such a Beloved
Who can bring news?
When one invokes God,
Gabriel the Messenger has no place in between.

There will be no questioning for him
Who from this world and the hereafter has retired;
Having abandoned all desire,
Of him interrogating angels have nothing to enquire.

There is no fear nor hope for him
Who abandons both richness and poverty,
His knowledge and his deeds
Are not weighed on the Scale.

It is but a marketplace, this Doomsday,
Each servant thinks anxiously "what will become of me?"
O *Yunus*, for the Lovers,
No Judgement Day will there be!

GLOSSARY OF TERMS

Abstention   *Riyada.* Abstention is the practice of refraining from the world in order to loosen the power of the self which hinders one from perceiving reality as it is.

Affliction   *Dard.* It refers to the Affliction of Love which is the outcome of separation from the Beloved. In this sense the Affliction is the very Remedy as it leads the Lover to seek joining with the Beloved, that is, God.

Alif   The first letter of the Arabic alphabet, which symbolizes Oneness and Essential Perfection, that is, God.

Association   *Shirk.* Association of partners with God.

Attainer to God *Eren.* Friend of God.

Azrael   The Angel of Death.

Beauty   *Jamal.* The Beauty of God. On the other hand, its opposite, Majesty *(Jalal)* denotes that which is other than God, that is, the world behind which God veils Himself. Troubles and trials come from the Majesty of God, whereas compassion and provisions come from His Beauty. The reality of Adam which is of divine form is the mirror of Divine Beauty. His bodily form, being a veil to this mirror, is the place of manifestation of Majesty.

Bewilderment   *Hayrah.* Shaykh al-Kashani says: "The ocean of *Hayrah* is the Unity pervading all and manifesting itself in multiple forms. It is bewildering because of the Unity appearing in a concrete determined form in every single thing and yet remaining non-determined in the whole. It is bewildering because it is non-limitation and limitation."

Breath	*Nafas, dam.* Spiritually 'breath' refers to the breath of the All-Merciful *(Nafas ar-Rahman).* It is the breath of the Perfect Man which revives dead hearts.
Buraq	A heavenly steed which transported the prophet Muhammad from Mecca to Jerusalem, and through the heavens during the *Isra* and *Mi'raj* or "Night Journey".
Cup	*Ka's, qadah.* The words of the Guide which are words of Gnosis. The seeker, hearing them, becomes intoxicated with delight. It may also refer to the Heart of the Lover, thirsty for Divine Love.
Cup-bearer	*Saaki.* The Guide who serves the Wine of Divine Love to the Lovers.
Dajjal	Antichrist. The appearance of *Dajjal* is one of the major signs of the Day of Judgement.
Drop	*Qatra. Zerre.* This term is used in the pairing of drop/ocean. Here the drop refers to the manifoldness of reality in which one perceives himself as distinct from others and from God, with the illusion that he exists by himself. So the drop refers to the illusory self which has to be overcome through dissolving itself into the Ocean of Oneness where it belongs. [See *Ocean*].
Drunk	*Esrik, mast.* [See *Wine*]
Duality	Duality is affirming the existence of the creation which is separate from the Existence of God, and this is nothing but *shirk*, that is, associating another existence with God, as Muhyiddin Ibn Arabi plainly explains in *The Treatise on Ahadiyya*. On the other hand, Jalalludin Rumi refers to such a perception, which is common for ordinary people, as 'cross-eyedness'.
Face	*Wajh.* Face is one's essential reality. It also refers to the Beauty of God. The self *(nafs)* being the veiling of the Face of God, has to be removed to see His Beauty.
Fard	Obligatory deeds in Islam.

Ferhad	A lover famous in Eastern story. He loved Shirin, who was the wife of King Khosru. He was a sculptor, and renowned throughout Persia. The King, fearing his rivalry, tried to divert his mind from his passion, and sought to find for him some impossible task. As Shirin had demanded a "river of milk," he was bidden to clear away the rocks obstructing the passage of the great mountain of Beysitoun, and to cause the rivers on the opposite sides of the mountain to join. Ferhad agreed on condition that, if he were successful, Shirin should be given to him. For years he laboured, and carved out wonderful caverns. Only a few days' work remained to be done, when the King heard reports that the project was succeeding: he thereupon sent a messenger to tell Ferhad that Shirin was dead. On hearing this, Ferhad died, some say by killing himself with his axe, others say by throwing himself over a precipice.
Feridun	An Iranian mythical king and hero who is an emblem of victory, justice and generosity in Persian literature.
Four Books	The Four Books are Zaboor, the Pentateuch, the Gospel and the Koran, which were revealed to David, Moses, Jesus and Muhammad respectively. These four books refer to the four stations of understanding God. These are the unification of the Names, the unification of the Acts, unification of the Attributes and the unification of the Essence. Therefore, the Koran represents the Essence; the Pentateuch, the self-manifestation of the Attributes; Zaboor, the self-manifestation of the Acts; and, the Gospel, the self-manifestation of the Names. All of these Four Books are gathered in Alif, the first letter of the Arabic alphabet, which symbolizes Oneness and Essential Perfection, that is, God.
Friend	*Dost.* 'Friend' implies both the Perfect Man and God who is the true Beloved.
Friend of God	*Eren. Er.* A spiritually realized person.
Geyikli Hasan	A friend of God who lived in Anatolia in the time of Yunus Emre.
Guide	*Murshid.* The spiritual guide or master who leads the seeker to God.

Haman	The vezier to Pharaoh at the time of prophet Moses. Referring to Moses as a sorcerer and a liar, Pharaoh and Haman rejected Moses' call to worship God and refused to set the children of Israel free.
Hamza	A heroic epic figure in Iranian literature.
Hasan	One of the grandsons of the Prophet Muhammad.
Hawk	*Dogan.* Hawk, symbolizing a spiritual Guide.
Heart	*Gonul.* The Heart is the perfect place of the self-manifestation of God. It is the Heart where the Hidden Treasure is present. It is the Throne of God. Ibn Arabi states: "My heart has become capable of every form: it is a pasture for gazelles and a convent for Christians, and a temple for idols and the pilgrims' Kaaba and the tables of the Torah, and the book of the Koran. I follow the religion of Love: whatever way Love's camels take, that is my religion and faith."
Hoori	The word *Hoori* refers to heavenly angels, splendid beings, or celestial virgins who await the saved in paradise after death.
Huseyn	One of the grandsons of the Prophet Muhammad.
Imam	An Islamic leader, often the leader of worship in the mosque and the Muslim community.
Intellect	*Aql.* The intellect has only a restricted understanding of the Truth. If a man is a servant of his Lord he renders his intellect unto Him. However, if he is the servant of his own speculation, he reduces the Truth to the partial judgement of his intellect.
Intercede	*Shefaat.* One of the attributes specific to the Prophet Muhammad whereby he has the authority to intercede on behalf of believers in the afterlife.
Jamaah	Literally this means "community," but is used to specifically refer to a community or group of Muslim believers who perform prayer behind the Imam.
Joseph	The Prophet Joseph.
Kauser	The *Hauzu'l-Kausar* is the lake or fountain of abundance in Heaven. Persons having crossed the *As-Sirāt* arrive at this lake, from which one is expected to drink in order to forget any bad experiences they may have had during their lives, before moving further into Heaven.

Laila	The goal of the spiritual quest is personified as a woman, usually named *Laila* which means 'night'. It symbolizes the Essence of God.
Language of Birds	*Kush dili.* The Koran states that the prophet Solomon *(Sulaiman)* understood the language of the birds and conversed with them. The language of birds was also granted to the prophet David.
Love	*Ishk, ashk.* For sufis, Love is nothing but Divine Love. They expressed the Journey to God in terms of a lover's seeking his beloved, since there is a great similarity between them, except one is carnal and ephemeral, the other, divine and everlasting.

In the beginning of the Journey, the Lover has the bitter consciousness of being separate from the Beloved. This separation from the Beloved is the Affliction the Lover suffers. This Affliction can only be healed by Joining the Beloved. So, the Affliction is itself the remedy, since only with this Affliction can the Lover join his Beloved. This separation causes great grief because of which he cries and wails, that being the heartfelt invocation of the Beloved. And he risks everything, even his soul, to join his Beloved.

True Love demands from the Lover that he lose himself in the Beloved. The existence of the Beloved takes such an important place in the existence of the Lover that nothing remains of him. Also everything loses its value and beauty before the Beloved. This situation is symbolized by the moth burning into the candle, or a drop merging with the ocean.

Thus through Love, through annihilation of his self or *nafs,* the Lover recognizes the true nature of existence and becomes a Gnostic. He sees the Beloved, God, ever-present in everything through the self-manifestation of His Names and Attributes. There is no way to recognize it without the annihilation of the self, and there can be no way to annihilate the self without Love.

However, while seemingly this is through the death of the self, it is actually an awakening from sleep. Indeed it is now we are dead, suffering the torments of the grave – the body.

Luqman	A wise man after which *Sura Luqman,* the thirty-first chapter of the Koran, was named.

Majnun A person who is insane or mentally incompetent. One who is lost in the Love of God.

Man of Poverty *Miskin.* The meaning of poverty is explained in the Koran: "O mankind! You are poor in your relation to God, while God is He Who is the All-Wealthy and Worthy of Praise" [35:15]. And the Prophet Muhammad, being the Perfect Man, states how he conceives of the essential poverty of his Manhood: "*Al-faqru fakhri* – Poverty is my glory."

One who is perfectly conscious of one's essential poverty before God and one's absolute dependence on Him abandons his illusory self, and as he sees that the One that acts in himself is God, he becomes Rich with God.

Mansion *Kiosk.* The mansions in the Heaven to which the Koran refers: "But those who heed their Lord will have mansions raised upon mansions high, beneath which running waters flow." (39:20)

Mihrab A semicircular niche in the wall of a mosque that indicates the *qibla*; that is, the direction of the Kaaba in Mecca and hence the direction that Muslims should face when praying.

Moth *Parwana.* The candle is the Absolute Beauty of God. The Lover, falling in love with the Beloved, constantly turns around Her like a moth until his existence is annihilated by the Fire of Love.

Mount Qaf It is believed that Qaf is a mountain range which encompasses the entire world.

Mustafa A title of the Prophet Muhammad which means 'Chosen' or 'Elect'.

Night of Power *Laila-i-Qadr.* The night when the Koran was first revealed.

Nightingale *Bulbul.* The nightingale symbolizes the Lover, where the Rose symbolizes the Beloved in traditional poetry. [See also *Rose*]

Nushirewan An illustrious king of Persia who reigned from A.D. 531 to A.D. 578.

Ocean *Darya, Umman.* The Ocean represents the Absolute Being of God. The waves of the Ocean stand for the becoming of the world of manifoldness, which has no existence in itself, being only the self-manifestation of the Absolute Being. Thus, Ocean stands for the World of Oneness. [See also *Drop*]

Other *Gayr. Ma siwa.* The phrase 'that which is other' refers to everything other than God.

Pearl *Durr.* The pearl symbolizes divine knowledge. In this symbolism gnostics are symbolized as being divers who harvest pearls in the depths of the ocean.

Pen *Qalam, Qalam-i Ala.* The first thing created by God. It gathers together all the realities of creation in itself. It is known as the Light of Muhammad or the First Intellect. From the Pen has been created the Tablet *(Lawh-i Mahfuz)* which is the detailing of what there is in the Pen, that is, all the realities of creation.

Perfect Man *Er.* Friend of God.

Qalu Bala God created the spirits of all people before He created the world and the beings in it. He brought them together in a place called the realm of spirits. Then, He brought all of them to His presence and asked them: "*Alastu birabbikum* – Am I not your Lord? The spirits answered: "*Qalu: Bala* – They said: Yes you are." The time when this conversation took place is called *Qalu Bala.*

Qarun Korah. He is mentioned in the Koran. He is recognized as rich, and became very arrogant due to his pride and ignorance *(The Koran, 28:76).*

Queen of Sheba *Bilqis.* A monarch of the ancient kingdom of Sheba. She, then married the prophet Solomon.

Rose *Gul.* The rose is the symbol of the Beloved.

Rose garden *Gulistan.* Oneness.

Rostam Rostam is a Persian hero mentioned in Ferdowsi's *Shahnameh.*

Sacrifice *Qurban.* The annihilation of the self for the sake of the Beloved, God.

Salah	*Salat.* Prayer. One of the five pillars of Islam.
Scale	*Terazu. Mizan.* A spiritual scale which will be used to weigh one's good deeds and sins in the Hereafter.
Selfish assertion	*Dava.* Assertion is a veil between God and his servant since the servant puts forth something which cannot be attributed to himself. It can also be understood as the pursuit of worldly cause.
Sharia	Divine Law. It is the outward aspect of Islam. Islam has three aspects: Divine Law *(Sharia),* the Way *(Tariqa)* and Reality *(Haqiqa).* The *Sharia* is the boat we all have to sail on, the *Tariqa* is the sea, and *Haqiqa* is the jewels and pearls we extract from the sea.
Sheikh Ibrahim	*Ibrahim Adham.* While he was the Sultan of Balh, he abandoned everything he had and became a dervish. He is widely used in sufi poems as a symbol of renunciation of the world for the sake of God.
Sohbet	A discourse given by a spiritual Guide.
Solomon	*Sulaiman.* A prophet mentioned both in the Bible and the Koran.
Sugar	*Sheker.* Sugar symbolizes Gnosis.
Sunnah	The deeds done and recommended by the Prophet Muhammad.
Tablet	*Lawh-i Mahfuz.* [See *Pen*]
Tapduk Emre	Yunus Emre's spiritual Guide on the path to God.
Tariqa	The inner aspect of Islam through which *haqiqa* and *marifah* are attained.
Throne	*Arsh.* The Throne is the Highest Heaven that includes all the worlds, spiritual or material, on which "the Merciful is established," [*The Koran*, 20:5]. In man, being a microcosmos, the Throne corresponds to the Heart. So in its true meaning the Throne is the Heart of the Perfect Man. "Neither My heaven nor My earth could contain Me, but the soft, humble heart of My believing servant can contain Me," indicates this. As the Throne is the highest point of the universe, the earth *(farsh)* is the lowest point.

Water of Life *Ab-i Hayat.* Essential self-manifestation of God.

Wine *Sharab, hamr, may.* Wine means the Gnosis of God, the outcome of which is Divine Love. "And their Lord will give to them to drink of a Wine Pure and Holy," [*The Koran*, 76:21].